123796
JB De Leeuw, A.L.
C548d George Rogers Clark.
MISSOURI RIVER REGIONAL LIBRARY
Osage County Library Service Center
Linn, Missouri 65051
THOMAS JEFFERSON LIBRARY SYSTEM

The Discovery Books are prepared
under the educational supervision of

Mary C. Austin, Ed.D.
Reading Specialist and
Professor of Education
Western Reserve University

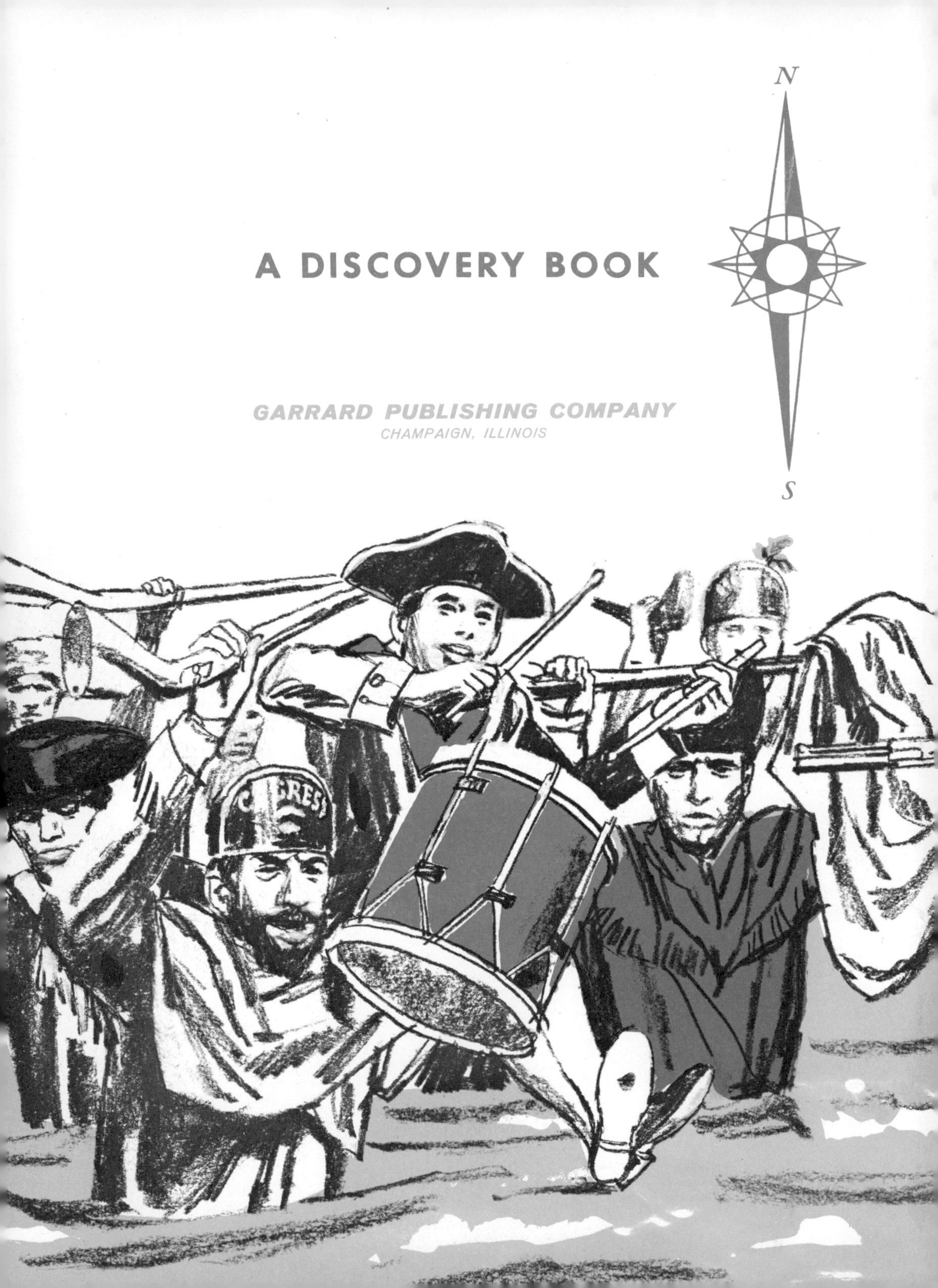

A DISCOVERY BOOK

GARRARD PUBLISHING COMPANY
CHAMPAIGN, ILLINOIS

George Rogers Clark

Frontier Fighter

by Adèle deLeeuw

illustrated by Russ Hoover

To Edward Blair Bennett III

Library of Congress Catalog Card Number: 67-10098

Contents

George Rogers Clark: Frontier Fighter

Chapter 1

Red-Haired George

"George!" The schoolmaster's voice was stern. "Keep your eyes on your book!"

George Rogers Clark looked down at the page in front of him. It was spring in the year 1764, and he was twelve years old. He wanted to be out-of-doors, hunting or fishing or riding through the woods.

"I like books well enough," he told his brother Jonathan when they were walking home together. "I like to learn.

But there are plenty of things to learn that aren't in books."

"Yes," Jonathan agreed. "And you know many of them."

George was glad that Jonathan had said that. He was proud of the way he could walk through the woods, as silent as any Indian. The stars at night were his friends, and he could name them. He could imitate squirrels and bob-whites. He could throw a knife into a tree trunk from a distance, and shoot straight with a rifle.

"Look!" George suddenly cried out. "There's a little green heron!"

Jonathan could not find it. "Where?"

"On the grass near the riverbank."

Jonathan sighed. "You have eyes like a hawk."

"But no hawk has red hair," George said, laughing.

"You know the saying in the Clark family," Jonathan reminded him. "Any Clark with red hair is bound to be outstanding."

"It's something to live up to," George admitted.

They walked slowly toward the snug farmhouse, nestled in the green fields. The family had lived in Caroline County, Virginia, since George was five. He remembered how they had moved east from their farm at the foot of the Blue Ridge Mountains. His mother was happier here. It was a great deal safer, she had said. But George missed the wild country and the blue hills rising against the sky.

Someday he would go back and see what lay beyond them. For years the British had fought the French for the land to the west. Now Britain had won the war, and the country belonged to the British.

People were moving west every day. Trappers brought tales of the rich country and beautiful rivers. The settlers from the east wanted to claim the land for their families.

When he was nineteen, George made up his mind to leave home. The Clark family was growing. George had five brothers now, including the new baby, William. William had red hair, too. There were also four sisters in the household.

George decided to make his own way.

He told his father of his plans. John Clark looked at his tall, broad-shouldered son. "Every young man," he said, "needs to do what he feels he must do. How will you make your living, George?"

"By surveying," George answered promptly. "You taught me how. And I have Grandfather's instruments. There will be plenty of land to measure for other people. Perhaps I'll find some to mark for my own!"

Chapter 2

A Taste of War

After several trips George Rogers Clark found some beautiful land to claim for his own. It lay along Fish Creek, a stream that flowed into the Ohio River. Here he spent the fall of 1772, chopping down trees and clearing the ground. He hunted and fished and surveyed his property.

He discovered a mound full of Indian graves. Buried with the Indians were many of their belongings, their pottery and tools. Clark had always been interested in Indians. He studied the things with care.

Sometimes a trapper came by, and they ate supper together. They cooked on a campfire outside the shelter Clark had built for himself. Sometimes he went to the cabin of his nearest neighbor, four miles away. There were children in that household. He taught them their ABC's during the winter. He wished his old schoolteacher could see him now!

When spring came, he planted corn. Then he put his belongings in a canoe he had shaped from a big poplar log.

He explored 170 miles down the Ohio River. To the north lay the Indian country. To the south lay Kentucky, which was just being settled. He went as far as Big Sandy River and then turned back.

His camp was still there, and the corn was as high as his waist. Someone offered a fine price for his land, but George was in no hurry to sell. His property would be worth much more as time went on. That winter he hunted and trapped and took the furs to trading posts. Sometimes he surveyed land for his neighbors. People began to know him up and down the river.

One of Clark's friends was Logan, chief of the Mingo Indians. Logan had been given the name of a white man.

Clark often stayed with the Mingos. He learned the language and ways of the Indians.

Chief Logan taught him a cure for rattlesnake bite. "Take the root of the pocoon plant," Chief Logan said. "Mash the root and put it on the bite." Clark respected the Indians for their knowledge of nature. He had always been interested in plants himself.

One day a white man was killed by a band of Cherokee Indians. Some of the settlers then wanted to raid Chief Logan's camp in return. George would not let them. "Logan shared his food and fire with me," he said. "His tribe played no part in the killing."

One of the white men would not listen. His name was Daniel Greathouse.

He was a lazy man who made money selling rum to the Mingos.

Greathouse met some Indians from Logan's camp. He led them to a dark hut and gave them rum. Then he killed them all. They were Chief Logan's closest relatives. Logan swore revenge. He called on other tribes to help him. Soon there was fighting all over the countryside.

George felt sorry for Chief Logan, but he knew the settlers had to defend themselves from Indian attacks. An army had to be formed. Clark went up and down the river, getting men for the militia. "He's a born leader," the men said. "He's young, and he has a good head on his shoulders." They elected Clark a senior captain in the militia.

Lord Dunmore, the British governor of Virginia, came with a regiment to help. After bloody battles the Indians were finally ready to make peace.

Clark had proved himself a fine officer during the fighting. "Why don't you join the British army?" Lord Dunmore asked.

Clark shook his head. He loved the wild life of the frontier too much to leave it. Besides, Virginia and the other colonies were having trouble with Britain. Britain was taxing them unfairly and making laws they did not like. If Clark had to fight for anyone, it would be for America, not Britain.

Clark was asked to survey lands in Kentucky. So he started west. He was anxious to see the rich Kentucky lands that everyone was talking about.

Chapter 3

A Mission to Williamsburg

"Welcome to Harrodsburg!" James Harrod held out his hand to the tall, red-haired traveler.

Harrodsburg was a group of cabins surrounded by a stockade. Beyond the stockade lay the settlers' fields. Beyond the fields rose the forest through which Clark had traveled. The fields were rich, and the forest was full of game.

"How do you like Kentucky?" James Harrod asked.

"It's the most beautiful country I've seen," Clark replied with enthusiasm.

"Then I hope you'll stay with us."

James's brother, Will, came out of his cabin. He was a big man with a black beard. The brothers were proud of their settlement.

"This is fine country," James said. "We want to stay here. But we have had a lot of trouble with the Indians. They set fire to some of our cabins. The Indians think of Kentucky as their hunting grounds. We're not welcome."

Clark made Harrodsburg his headquarters while he traveled all around Kentucky. As he surveyed land, he visited the other settlements and their stockades. He wanted to find out how the people felt.

People in the settlements always told the same story—there was trouble with the Indians.

There was trouble about land claims, too. Often settlers who had bought land from a company found that they did not own it at all. The Indians believed the land belonged to them, and they had not sold it to the pioneers. That caused trouble, and there were no courts to settle quarrels.

England still ruled all the colonies, but England was far away.

"Kentucky should govern herself!" Clark said strongly. "Virginia and the other colonies have courts of law. We need to have our own courts of law, so that we will be able to settle these matters for ourselves."

Meanwhile, the colonists in the East were growing angry. England passed new tax laws that were a burden. "We want justice! We want freedom from Britain!" they shouted.

News of these problems reached Kentucky. "Things have gone from bad to worse," Clark told James Harrod. "There's even talk of war."

It was more than talk. The news came. The Revolutionary War between Britain and her colonies had begun!

The war began along the east coast. "It may spread here before long. The British have already stirred up the Indians," James Harrod told Clark. "We've got to be prepared. We've got to get powder for our guns. But we have no money to pay for the powder."

Clark had been thinking about the problem. "I have a plan," he said. "Let's call the people together."

People came to Harrodsburg from all the other settlements in Kentucky. "We will need help," Clark said, "if the war comes to Kentucky. As we are just west of Virginia, perhaps we can become a part of Virginia. Then the Virginians will give us ammunition and supplies."

The Kentucky settlers thought this was a good idea. They voted to send Clark to Williamsburg, the capital of Virginia.

Clark set out at once. It would be a long hard trip—700 miles! And there would be danger from Indians all along the way. But Clark was not worried. He knew how to survive in the wilderness.

Chapter 4

Five Hundred Pounds of Powder

There was very exciting news in Williamsburg. The British governor, Lord Dunmore, had been chased out of town. "We have an American governor now—Patrick Henry," they told Clark.

Clark met with Patrick Henry and the Executive Council of Virginia. "We must have supplies and ammunition now in order to fight the British," Clark said. "Remember, we'll protect you from the Indians in return."

The Council promised to give Kentucky 500 pounds of gunpowder. It would be shipped as far as Fort Pitt, a frontier town on the Ohio River. From there the gunpowder would have to be carried by boat.

Clark wrote James Harrod. He asked for boatmen to meet him at Fort Pitt.

While he waited for a reply, he visited his family. His parents and sisters were overjoyed to see him. All of his brothers except little William were away, fighting the British.

Little William was delighted to have a big brother at home. He listened wide-eyed to Clark's stories of Kentucky. His cousin, Joseph, listened too. Joseph was a fine, strong boy in his teens.

"Take me with you," Joseph begged.

"You're much too young," Clark said.

"I'm sixteen. My folks don't mind. All the boys I know are fighting. If you don't take me with you, I'll join another company."

Clark thought it over. Then he said, "In a couple of weeks I'll reach Fort Pitt. You can meet me there."

Clark went back to Williamsburg. James Harrod had not answered his letter asking for boatmen. Finally Clark could wait no longer. In the middle of the winter he set off for Fort Pitt.

When he reached Fort Pitt, the first person he met on the dock was his cousin Joseph Rogers. "I've been here for weeks," Joseph grinned. "And I've brought you some money that your father sent for you."

"Fine! I really need it," said Clark.

Clark hired a boat and a crew. He used his own money. It was snowing when they loaded the little flat-bottomed boat and set off down the river. It was bitter cold but they dared not build a fire on board. They were afraid that the Indians might see them.

The Indians did see them. One of the boatmen suddenly cried out, "Look! They're following us in canoes!"

"Indians!" Clark said. The canoes were light and fast. Their own boat was slow and clumsy. They could not win the race against the Indians.

Clark thought quickly. "We must try to make it to Limestone Creek. There are caves in the riverbank. We can hide the powder kegs in the caves."

That was their only chance. The men poled furiously. But the Indians were gaining on them. Finally Clark's party reached the creek. The men worked madly, rolling the kegs up the bank to the caves. Then they rushed back to their boat. Each man grabbed a pole, and they swung the boat out into the river again.

Then they reached a point of land, grounded their boat, and waded ashore. Soon they could hear the Indians yelling behind them. "They've got our boat," Clark said. "But we're safe."

It was 90 miles to Harrodsburg from where they were. Clark knew a path that followed an old buffalo trail. On the way they met Simon Kenton, a man from Harrodsburg. He had a deer steak.

He had been on a hunting trip. It was Christmas Eve. They roasted the deer meat and enjoyed a fine feast.

Clark and Kenton decided to go back to Harrodsburg to get help. Joseph Rogers and the other men would stay hidden deep in the woods until they came back.

James Harrod met Clark at the stockade. "George! I thought you were lost!"

"Didn't you get my letter asking for men to go after the gunpowder?"

"No. I'll round up the men and go after the powder. You get some sleep."

Before Harrod started out, Clark awakened to find a man standing at his door. It was one of the boatmen. His face was caked with blood.

"Bad news, Clark. Some of the men thought they could move the powder by themselves. They ran right into a nest of Shawnees. Four men were shot."

"What about Joseph?" Clark asked, his face pale.

"He was captured. But the powder's still safe in the caves."

Clark tried not to imagine what might happen to his young cousin. He put on his boots and picked up his rifle. "Find Harrod," he cried. "Tell him I'm going with him. I'm going to make sure that powder gets to Kentucky!"

Chapter 5

Secret Orders

Clark and Harrod brought the gun-powder safely back to Harrodsburg. Then they sent messages to the other settlements in Kentucky.

"Virginia has agreed to all we asked for," Clark said. "We can be a county of Virginia and make some of our own laws."

The people of Kentucky formed their own militia. They made Clark a major. He was only twenty-four years old.

Clark and his men would have the job of guarding the settlements in the wilderness.

That year 1777 was called "The Year of the Bloody Sevens" in Kentucky. The Indians were raiding the settlements again. The British were supplying them with guns and ammunition.

The British wanted to frighten the settlers and make them give up their land. Workers were scalped in their fields. Cattle were stolen. People were afraid to plant their crops. Something had to be done now. The militia was not large enough to defend the whole frontier.

As Clark traveled from fort to fort, he made a plan. Then he set out for Williamsburg to see Patrick Henry.

There he learned exciting news. Men from the thirteen colonies had held a meeting. They declared that the thirteen colonies were free from Britain, and that they were a new nation—the United States of America! The flag of the union had been designed. It had thirteen red and white stripes and thirteen white stars on a blue field.

Patrick Henry was glad to see Clark. Clark told him about the Indian raids.

"The British up in Detroit are giving guns to the Indians. Colonel Hamilton is called the 'Hair Buyer.' He pays a good sum for every American scalp that the Indians bring him. One of these days Hamilton will come down with his army and attack us. We must attack him first."

"How will you do that, Major?"

Clark's blue eyes shone. "The British have soldiers at Cahokia and Kaskaskia and Vincennes. Those are forts in the Illinois country. They were French forts in the old days. The settlers are French. We will attack the forts and take the soldiers by surprise. I have had spies at each of the forts. They have brought me reports. We can do it, sir, if we have men and money."

Patrick Henry cried, "It's a splendid plan! But I must talk it over with the others. I'll have an answer for you in two weeks."

Those were the longest two weeks Clark ever spent. Finally, Patrick Henry sent for him. Clark was promised some money and 350 men.

Clark tried not to show how disappointed he was. He needed twice as much money and twice as many men. But General Washington needed men too. The fighting was not going well in the East. Washington was now at Valley Forge. He was trying to build up his army.

"I will give you two sets of orders," Patrick Henry told Clark. "One will give you permission to take troops to protect Kentucky. The other will permit you to march on the British forts. That order must be kept secret. Show it only to your captains. No one else must know about it. You must be able to take the forts by surprise. And from now on, you will be *Colonel* Clark. Good Luck!"

Clark wrote letters to his captains in Kentucky. They were to round up as many men as they possibly could. Then they were to meet him at the Monongahela River.

The men his captains brought were farmers. They wore fur caps and shirts of deerskin. Their moccasins were old and dirty. They carried short-handled axes, rifles, and long-bladed knives.

"Well," Clark thought, "at least they are young and strong. But there are only 150 of them!"

They loaded the flatboats at Fort Pitt. Then they started down the Ohio River toward the Falls of the Ohio. This was a dangerous stretch of water, full of stones and rapids. They camped at Corn Island above the Falls.

While they were there, a messenger brought good news. France had decided to join the United States in her fight for freedom!

Clark cheered. "Now that France is helping us, we have a better chance to win the war," he thought.

He called his men together. He could tell them now about the secret orders. "The tide of the war is turning," he said. "We are not going to Kentucky to *defend* it. We are going into northwest country held by the British. We are going to *attack*! First we attack the fort at Kaskaskia. After that, we capture Cahokia. Then we will take the forts at the other towns. Are you all coming with me?"

"Aye, aye!" they shouted.

On June twenty-fourth they started down the river from Corn Island. Suddenly the skies grew gray. The sun disappeared. The men thought it was a bad omen. But Clark was delighted. Now the Indians would not see them passing! It was an eclipse of the sun.

"This is a good sign!" he cried happily. "It is a sign that all will go well."

Chapter 6

Captured Without a Shot

After four days on the river, they met a party of men in a big canoe. Clark's men covered them with their rifles. "Come aboard!" Clark ordered.

He thought the men might be spies. But they were hunters who had been to Kaskaskia. This was a real piece of luck. Clark got more information about the town and the fort that protected it.

The hunters thought Kaskaskia could be taken by surprise.

Now Clark changed his plans. Instead of going directly to the town by way of the river, they would go by land.

The men marched through thick forests. Clark noted all the trees and mosses to add to his fund of nature lore. The more he saw of this land, the more impressed he was. He must win the Illinois country for the United States!

Finally they came to a grassy plain. They did not know which way to go. One of the hunters said he knew of a path. Clark ordered him to lead. The man lost his way. Clark was afraid the Indians would find them in this open country. Perhaps the man was a spy after all!

"Find the path at once, or you will be shot," he said sternly.

After an hour's searching the frightened man led them onto the hunter's trail. They marched all day with nothing to eat. At last toward dark, they came to a high place. And below them was the Kaskaskia River. Across the river lay a peaceful village, protected by its fort.

When evening fell, Clark went to a farmhouse near the river. "Get me enough rowboats for my army!" he ordered the farmer. After dark his army rowed quietly across the river.

"I'm dividing you into two parties," Clark said. "One group will climb the bank to the fort gate that faces the river. The other group will surround the town."

Clark himself led the men swiftly up the high riverbank. Just then, the town dogs began to bark. The men froze in their tracks. At last the dogs stopped, and they moved on. There was no sentry at the gate. Like shadows, Clark's men crept across the fort yard.

Voices sounded. Suddenly a dozen British soldiers rushed out into the darkness. Clark's men fell upon them. Clark grabbed a lantern and led the way to the governor's house.

Governor Philippe de Rocheblave was sound asleep. Clark shook him awake. De Rocheblave stared up at him under his nightcap. "I am George Rogers Clark," he said. "You have just become a prisoner of the Commonwealth of Virginia."

Then the rest of Clark's army ran through the town. They shouted and whooped. The frightened villagers cowered in their homes. "Stay inside until daybreak on pain of death!" they were told.

Clark's men patrolled the streets. No one could get away. No messenger could creep out to run for help.

Kaskaskia had fallen to the Americans! Not a shot had been fired. Not a drop of blood had been spilled. It was July 4, 1778, just two years after the Declaration of Independence had been signed.

Chapter 7

Two Belts of Wampum

Father Gibault, the village priest, came to see Clark. Colonel Clark was dirty and scratched. His red hair was matted. He looked very forbidding.

"I have come to ask if the people of Kaskaskia may gather in the church," the priest said. "They may never see one another again. They wish to pray and say farewell."

Clark said gruffly, "They may gather, if they wish. But they may not leave town." Clark had trained himself to appear harsh. He was young for a colonel. He wanted to seem older. He knew many lives would be saved if the people respected him and did not rebel.

Father Gibault came back to see Clark an hour later. Now Clark was bathed and dressed in fresh clothes. "The families here expect you will send them into exile. They hope that parents and children will not be separated. The people know little about the war, sir. They are still Frenchmen. They bear America no ill will."

Before this, Clark had not dared to be too kind. But now he knew how the people felt, and he could be generous.

"I have news for you," he said. "France is sending men and money to help us. She believes in our fight for liberty."

When the Kaskaskians heard this, there was joy everywhere. Clark said they were free to choose between Britain or the United States. All the Kaskaskians wanted to become a part of the United States. Clark had won them to his side! Father Gibault and Clark shook hands.

That same day Clark sent a troop of men to Cahokia. It was a trading town 50 miles away. Hunters and trappers and Indians came there from all over the Illinois country.

Some of the men from Kaskaskia went with Clark's soldiers. They told the Cahokians that they could become Americans if that was what they wished.

The people shouted, "Liberty! Liberty!" The Cahokians became Americans too. Not a drop of blood was shed!

Clark was pleased. "Now I must take Fort Sackville at Vincennes," he said. Vincennes was 200 miles away on the Wabash River. Here the British gave guns and ammunition to the Indians who raided Kentucky. Vincennes must be captured.

Father Gibault knew Vincennes well. He often preached there. Now he asked Clark, "Let me go to Vincennes ahead of your soldiers. The governor has gone to Detroit. If I talk to the citizens, they may join you against the British. Fighting may not be necessary. Let me try."

Two weeks later he returned. He had won the people of Vincennes!

He had other good news. "The Indian chiefs along the Wabash want to smoke the pipe of peace with you," Father Gibault reported. "They call you the 'Big Knife' commander."

Clark was delighted. He sent Leonard Helm and a small troop of men to take charge of Vincennes. Leonard Helm was one of Clark's friends from Harrodsburg. He was brave and gay and very popular with the soldiers.

Clark went to Cahokia and waited for the Indians to visit him. At the end of the summer they arrived. Clark rode out to the plains beyond Cahokia. As far as he could see, the land was dotted with Indian tents and campfires. The Indians could wipe out his tiny army in an hour if they wanted to!

He must use all he had learned of Indian ways.

Clark called all the Indians to a council. He held up two belts of wampum. One was blood-red. One was white. "I carry in my right hand war, and peace in my left." He told them why the Americans were fighting the British. Then he threw the belts down on the grass.

"Choose!" he cried.

The Indians talked all night and far into the next day. Then they picked up the white belt and trampled on the red one.

The Indians were his friends. And best of all, the entire Illinois country now belonged to the United States!

Chapter 8

The Guns Roared a Salute

It was late January in 1779. A sentry came to Colonel Clark's office at Cahokia. "Colonel Francis Vigo to see you, sir."

The little dark-haired Spanish merchant was a trader from St. Louis. He had traveled all around the prairie towns.

"I bring bad news," he said. "Colonel Hamilton came from Detroit with an army of 800 men. They captured Vincennes. Captain Helm and his men are prisoners. In the spring Hamilton plans to march on you here."

Clark paced back and forth. Poor Helm! Somehow he must think of a way to attack and take Hamilton by surprise.

How could he do it? The Wabash had overflowed, and the prairies were flooded. How could he get an army to Vincennes?

"We'll wade," Clark said to himself. "We'll swim. And we'll start at once!" They would be greatly outnumbered by the British. He was sure that a surprise attack was the only way to recapture the fort.

Clark called his captains together. He quickly outlined his plans. The captains were doubtful at first. Then they said, "We took Kaskaskia by surprise. We must make it work again."

Some of the Frenchmen at Kaskaskia volunteered to go. Clark borrowed money and bought a flatboat, the *Willing*. On it he mounted six small cannon. He filled the cabin with supplies. Forty men, under Captain John Rogers, marched aboard. They would go down the Mississippi River, up the Ohio River, and then up the Wabash. There they would wait with the supplies for Clark's army of 130 men to cross the prairie.

The women of Kaskaskia gave Clark flags they had sewed. They gave the men blankets and mittens. Father Gibault prayed for the army's success.

"There's a little boy outside who wants to go along," Captain Bowman told Clark. "He plays the drum. His parents will let him go, if you will take him."

Clark thought a moment. "Tell him to come along."

As soon as they started, it began to rain. It rained day and night. They plodded through mud, hour after hour. At dusk they made camp and slept in wet blankets. Before daylight they were on the march again. It never stopped raining.

After eight days they reached the Little Wabash River. It had flooded the land for miles around. A third of Clark's army was sick with chills and fever. He ordered those who were able to cut down trees. Then they built a boat from the wood and Clark sent scouts ahead.

"Now we'll go on to Vincennes!" Clark said.

He held his rifle high and waded into the water. Those who could march followed him. The drummer boy sat on a sergeant's shoulders, playing his drum. The men began to sing.

For five long miles they waded and stumbled through the icy water. When the water was too high, the drummer boy used his drum as a raft. The men laughed at this and their spirits rose.

That night they camped on a little hill. Although there was very little food, Clark would not let the men shoot game. The sound of guns could give them away to the enemy. All the men had to eat was a handful of parched corn.

Finally they came to the Wabash River, but the *Willing* was not there.

Clark's men made camp and called it "Camp Hunger."

The next morning Clark again plunged into the water, singing a song. "This is the last march," he said. "We're nine miles from Vincennes. Once we capture the fort, we can rest."

The men struggled on, their arms around each other's shoulders to keep from sinking into the mud. When they made camp, they could see the fort that guarded Vincennes ahead of them.

The soldiers captured a French hunter from Vincennes. Clark questioned him.

"Cut young trees, and we will fasten our flags to them," Clark told his men. "We will march in a zigzag line, behind trees and bushes. The British will think we have many more men than we do."

When they neared the fort, the cannon roared. But the cannon could not point downward. The Americans waited until they were very close to the fort. Then they fired. All night the battle continued. They used the last of their powder.

Two Frenchmen crept out from the town. "Here is powder for your rifles!" they cried. "We buried it months ago."

In the morning Clark sent a message to Colonel Hamilton. "I order you to immediately surrender yourself up."

Hamilton replied, "We are not disposed to be awed into any action unworthy of British subjects."

The Americans began firing again. Hamilton asked for a three-day truce.

Clark sent back an answer, "Meet me at the church with Captain Helm."

While Clark waited for a reply, a band of Indians came whooping toward the town. They carried American scalps that were still bloody. Clark captured the Indians and had them tomahawked.

This was a bold act. The British were frightened, and the gates of the fort opened. Colonel Hamilton came out with Captain Helm. "We will surrender," Hamilton said.

Next morning at ten o'clock the British soldiers marched out of the fort. The tired, muddy Americans marched in. "From this day on," said Clark, "this will be called Fort Patrick Henry."

The roar of a thirteen-gun salute began. That would be one for each of the thirteen stars of the American flag now floating over Vincennes.

Chapter 9

Joe Is Found

The *Willing* arrived three days later. It had been delayed by terrible storms. "How we hated to miss the fighting!" Captain Rogers cried. "You did a wonderful job. Now you have all the Illinois country under control."

"Yes, but now we must take Detroit," Clark said. "If we can take that fort, the whole Northwest Territory would be ours."

Patrick Henry promised Clark 500 fresh soldiers. They would join him in the spring. This was cheering news. But it meant that Clark would have to wait until spring to start his attack. It was hard for him to wait. He had great dreams for the new nation. He wanted it to be as large and strong as possible. And he wanted a part in making these dreams come true.

Clark never did go to Detroit. The Indians started attacking again all along the frontier. Clark traveled about and strengthened the forts. He built up Fort Nelson at the Falls of the Ohio River. Around it he helped to lay out the town of Louisville, Kentucky.

"It will be the most beautiful city in the United States," he said.

By now the Americans felt sure they would win the war against the British. The British were losing battles in the east. To make up for their losses there, the British encouraged the Indians in the west. The Indian attacks grew more and more severe.

In August the Indians were at a town called Piqua. Clark rushed there with his troops and surrounded the Indians. In the heat of battle a man dashed out of the fort. His face was painted, and his hair was tied in a tuft. American soldiers swiftly aimed at him with their rifles.

The man cried, "Don't shoot! Don't shoot! I'm an American!"

Clark looked hard. "Joe!" he cried. "Joseph Rogers!"

But a rifleman had already shot him. Joe fell forward. Clark bent over his cousin. Joe was dying. "I . . . spent four years . . . with the Shawnees," he gasped. "Now I was coming back, at last. Write to my folks, will you, George?"

Clark felt like weeping. At last Joe had been found, but too late.

Chapter 10

"To Her Beloved Son"

The Revolution was now over. The Americans had won. In 1785 there were few Indian raids. Clark sent for his family to come to Louisville.

He could not get over how young William had grown. William was strong and tall, with hair as red as his brother's.

The land Clark had chosen for his family sloped to the river. It was full of mulberry trees in bloom. His mother cried happily, "It's beautiful! We'll call it Mulberry Hill."

The family built a house there, and Clark lived with them for many years. He could watch the river from his tiny porch. In his spare time he read and studied nature.

The years of peace turned out to be disappointing years for Clark. During the war, he had paid for many of his army supplies himself. Now the state of Virginia was unable to pay him back. Most of Clark's land was seized to pay his debts.

But two wonderful things did happen. Clark's brother William joined the army. President Jefferson sent William Clark with Meriwether Lewis to explore the land beyond the Mississippi River. They went over the Rockies and all the way to the Pacific Ocean!

George Rogers Clark himself was famous, even though he was poor. When he was an old man, a group of citizens came to call on him. Across his lap they laid a beautiful sword. On its blade were the words: "Presented by the State of Virginia to her beloved son George Rogers Clark, who by the conquest of Illinois and St. Vincennes, extended her empire and aided in the defense of her liberties."

Today a marble dome stands on the Wabash River. It is held up by sixteen columns. Around the walls are murals showing the conquest of the West. In the center of the room is a tall bronze statue of George Rogers Clark. He is looking out over the Northwest Territory he won for his country.